I Love You Every Second

By Sandra A. Hinds
Illustrated by Casey G.

AuthorHouse™
1663 Liberty Drive
Bloomington, IN 47403
www.authorhouse.com
Phone: 1-800-839-8640

Published by AuthorHouse 04/29/2012

ISBN: 978-1-4567-2418-4 (sc)

Library of Congress Control Number: 2011900074

Any people depicted in stock imagery provided by Thinkstock are models
and such images are being used for illustrative purposes only.
Certain stock imagery © Thinkstock.

This book is printed on acid-free paper.

authorHOUSE®

Author's Thanks and Dedications

To Abba, thank you for this book—indeed, it is a wonderful gift.

To Raesa, my sweet inspiration for this labor of love. I love you.

To Ray and Marcus, my heart is full of love for you.

To Alma "Dean York" Foggo-York, you loved much and you were very much loved.

To all the children of the world and your loving caregivers, may love fill every area of your lives.

Illustrator's Dedication

To Lucien

Acknowledgments

I would like to thank Casey Girard for creating the beautiful illustrations for my words, Pierre Huberson for writing a wonderful song for the book, and Mary Ann André, Sharon Batson, Michele Caterina, Stephanie Cooper, Debra Lynn Goins, Kendra Stanton Lee, and Dr. Hyveth Williams for their support of this project. Special thanks go to the Diamond, Drake, Girard, Gouvea, Kharbanda, and Manalang families, as well as to Eva Komaridis, for being part of this book. Your love shines through on each page. This book is my dream come true and it is filled with LOVE. Thank you all for coming along on the journey with me—it has been a wonderful experience.—SAH

Introduction

Dear caregiver, parent, and reader:

Why are so many people in our culture plagued by feelings of emptiness and alienation? One answer, I believe, is that far too many of us were raised without loving caregivers and had to hide our feelings, needs, and memories as children. Another answer, I think, is that our society spends more time and other resources in training people to be professionals than we do in teaching them to be healthy, loving parents. As a result, our generation desperately tried to win their caregivers' love and worked overly hard to meet their parents' expectations. We want different relationships with our children.

This unpretentious little book is full of wisdom and powerful parenting perceptions that are presented in subtle ways. It aims to have an amazing impact on caregivers by deepening their understanding that:

- ♥ A child is a unique and precious gift who must be told that every day. He or she needs to know that there is no one like him or her anywhere on the earth.

- ♥ A child needs to be reassured and reminded with loving hugs and kisses that he or she is treasured.

- ♥ A child needs to be loved unconditionally.

- ♥ A child needs to know that he or she is special and wonderful.

- ♥ A child needs to hear positive words such as you are terrific, great, amazing, bright, and talented. Building a healthy self-esteem is critical in a child's development.

This is a work from the heart of a loving mother and caregiver, Sandra Hinds. This book seeks to enable those who practice its contents to raise children who grow up to love themselves, their families, friends, and neighbors.

I hope you will recommend this book to caregivers and organizations working with children. It will also make a great gift for your family and friends. That's how I, as an older parent, will put it to good use!

Dr. Hyveth Williams

Happy mother and grandmother

I love you every second.

I love you every minute.

I love you every hour.

I love you every day.

Sunday	Monday	Tuesday	Wednesday	Thursday	Friday	Saturday
1	2	3	4	5	6	7
8	9	10	11	12	13	14
15	16	17	18	19	20	21
22	23	24	25	26	27	28
29	30					

MONTH
week

I love you every week.

January February May March April June July August September October November December

I love you every month.

SPRING

SUMMER

I love you in every season.

FALL

WINTER

I love
you at
every
sunrise.

I love
you at
every
sunset.

I love you when the
sun is shining.

I love you when the
moon is glowing.

red orange yellow green blue indigo violet

I love you
when you
see a rainbow
in the sky.

I love you when
the stars are
shining bright.

I love you when
you are happy.

I love you when
you are sad.

I love you when you are laughing.

I love you when you are crying.

I love
you
when
you are
sleeping.

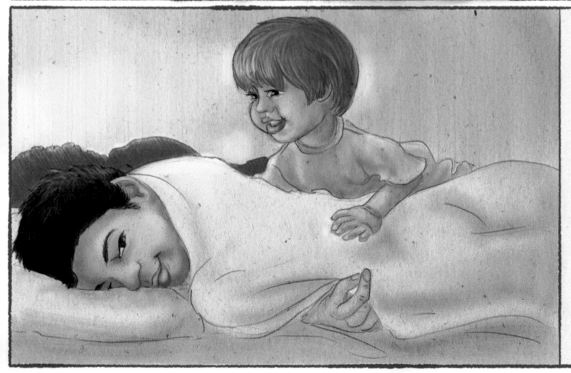

I love
you
when
you are
awake.

I love you when you are healthy.

I love you when you are sick.

I love you when
you are at home.

I love you when
you are at school.

I love
you
when
you are
playing.

I love
you
at quiet
time.

I love you when you are with your friends.

I love you when you are alone.

I love you at breakfast, lunch, snack time, and dinner.

I love you when
you are shy.

I love you when
you are angry.

I love you when
you are naughty.

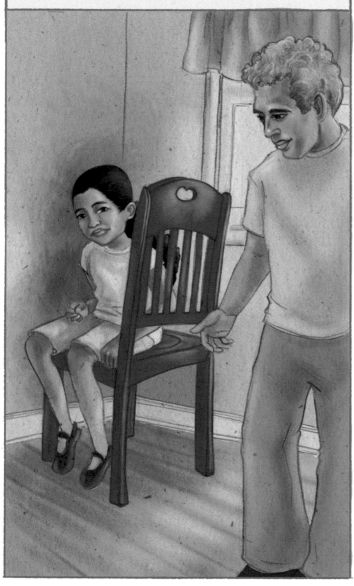

I love you when
you are nice.

I love you when you are far away.

I love you when you are close to me.

I love you now and forever.

You are VERY SPECIAL to me.

Love Lessons from Our Children

As parents and caretakers, we invest our love into our children. In return, we gain many "love lessons." These lessons often remind us what a privilege it is to be a part of a child's life. When some of the parents featured in this book were asked what they have learned from their children, they shared the following love lessons.

John and Lydia Diamond, an African-American couple, say they have learned much from their son, Baylor Holmes. "Baylor is our first and only child," Lydia says. "We would never have completely understood how very much a parent loves a child without him."

Steve and Kimber Lynn Drake say they cherish their daughters, Christina and Alyssa. Steve is Italian and Kimber Lynn is Japanese. When asked what she has learned from loving her children, Kimber Lynn says, "I have learned a lot about my own mother and my relationship with her. I was humbled and honored to realize that my mother could love me as deeply as I love my own children, and that I could mean as much to my children as my mother means to me."

Matt and Casey Girard say their son Lucien is the love of their lives. Matt describes himself as French Canadian, and Casey says she is "All American" with a heritage that includes Irish, Sicilian, Scottish, French, Hungarian, and American Indian-Cherokee. Matt says, "Being a parent means expanding your emotional range and experiencing boundless frustrations and limitless joys. Being a parent means playing like a kid again and people only think it is a 'little' strange." Casey says, "Loving my child has changed everything I ever believed in, making me more conscious of what I decide and how I act."

Valquiria and Wilson Gouvea hail from Brazil and enjoy being parents to Laura-Luiza. "We learned that wisdom, faith in God, and patience are essential in raising a child. We also learned that we didn't know we could love someone so much for who she is, regardless of anything."

Raynard and Sandra Hinds bring a rich racial and cultural heritage to how they raise Raesa Olivia Joyce and Marcus Lee. Raynard is African American and Sandra's cultural heritage is East and West Indian as well as Bermudian. "We have learned that our children are our most precious gifts. Loving them teaches us how to be more patient, kind, and compassionate," says Sandra.

Erica and Kevin Manalang say their children Case and Wednesday bring joy to their lives. Erica is Black Creole and Kevin is Filipino Irish. "From our children, we have learned the importance of patience and laughter. Though at times being a caregiver for a young child may be challenging, the reward is much greater," says Erica.

About the Author

Sandra A. Hinds considers herself to be an "island" lady. She was born on the island of Jamaica, grew up in Bermuda, and since living in Massachusetts, she has fallen in love with Martha's Vineyard. She received her Master's of Social Work degree from Boston University and has a deep passion for teaching. Sandra is very active in her church and community. She shares her life with her husband, Ray (her prince), and their children, Raesa and Marcus.

About the Illustrator

Casey Girard lives with her husband, Matt, and son, Lucien, in Boston, Massachusetts. She originally hails from a couple of Southern states, Kentucky and North Carolina. However, after realizing how much she loved snowy winters, she relocated to Massachusetts. She illustrates traditionally and digitally, and loves to explore new techniques. Children and animals are her favorite subjects to capture.

"Now and Forever"

The Power of Loving Words

Parents and Caregivers,

Use the final pages of this book to write loving words that describe your child. Read them to your child every day. Your words of love will serve as stepping stones in developing a positive self-esteem. Loving words go a long way and have lasting effects.

_____, you are **Wonderful, Smart, and Unique.**

Name of child

Printed in the United States
by Baker & Taylor Publisher Services